# OUR WORLD IN CRISIS

# IMMIGRATION

## CLAUDIA MARTIN

FRANKLIN WATTS
LONDON•SYDNEY

Franklin Watts
First published in Great Britain in 2018 by The Watts Publishing Group
Copyright © The Watts Publishing Group, 2018

Produced for Franklin Watts by
White-Thomson Publishing Ltd
www.wtpub.co.uk

ISBN: 978 1 4451 6375 8

Credits
Series Editor: Izzi Howell
Series Designer: Dan Prescott, Couper Street Type Co.
Series Consultant: Philip Parker

The publisher would like to thank the following for permission to reproduce their pictures:
Alamy: Images and Stories 10, AF Archive 13, DPA Picture Alliance 15, Joerg Boethling
27, Islandstock 30, Andrew Hasson 42; Walter Crane: 12; Getty: Christopher Morris 9;
Kamalthebest (with data from CIA World Factbook): 17t; Shutterstock: Janossy Gergely
cover, Huang Zheng 1 and 24, Nicolas Economou 2 and 21, westonjd 5t, Tang Yan Song
5b, Lucasz Z 6, Giannis Papanikos 11, Andrew V Marcus 14, A Aleksandravicius 17b, Rudy
Balasko 19, Thomas Koch 22, hikrcn 23, Jazzmany 25, Diego Mariottini 29, Andy Dean
Photography 31, Mikeledray 32, PongMoji 34, Tadeusz Ibrom 35, Nigel Spiers 36, Glynnis
Jones 37, Santeri Punnala 38, Ms Jane Campbell 39, Frederic Legrand, COMEO 41t, J
Stone 41b, Peter Braakmann 43, Riccardo Mayer 44, Samu Karhu 45.

All design elements from Shutterstock.

Every attempt has been made to clear
copyright. Should there be any
inadvertent omission please apply
to the publisher for rectification.

Printed in Singapore

Franklin Watts
An imprint of
Hachette Children's Group
Part of The Watts Publishing Group
Carmelite House
50 Victoria Embankment
London EC4Y 0DZ

An Hachette UK Company
www.hachette.co.uk
www.franklinwatts.co.uk

CONTENTS

# What is IMMIGRATION?

Immigration is when people arrive in a new country, intending to settle down and make a life there. People have many different reasons for leaving their home country, but they are nearly always looking for a better or safer life.

### Immigrant or emigrant?

An 'immigrant' is someone who arrives in a new country to live. In the country they are leaving, they are called an 'emigrant'. People who are on the move between one country and another are often called 'migrants'. To be considered an immigrant, someone must be intending to settle permanently in the new country. Tourists, who take brief trips abroad, are not immigrants. Commuters, who travel across a country border to work daily or weekly, are also not immigrants.

### Migrant or foreign worker?

Some people travel to another country to look for work for a short time, perhaps for the fruit-picking season. They are often called 'migrant workers'. Other people are invited to work in another country for a time, for example as builders on a construction project, or in an international business that arranges for them to work in an overseas office. These people are often called 'foreign workers' or 'guest workers'.

As migrant workers and foreign workers do not usually intend to make the new country their permanent home, they are not true immigrants, although they are often taken into account when considering statistics about immigration. The terms 'migrant worker' and 'foreign worker' are often used to mean the same people, while others use the term 'foreign worker' only to mean someone who takes up a more skilled job or is invited to work overseas.

## Illegal or undocumented immigrant?

Most countries have immigration laws, a set of rules about entering the country, and how people can gain the right to stay in the country legally. When someone enters a foreign country without having gone through the legal process, or tries to remain in a country without permission, they are often called an 'illegal immigrant'. Some people object to the term 'illegal immigrant' as it suggests that the person themself is illegal or bad, when in fact only the method they used to enter the country was illegal. They suggest that a term like 'undocumented immigrant' is used instead, expressing the fact that the immigrant does not have the right legal documents to remain in the country.

A foreign worker oversees a construction project in the United Arab Emirates.

Travellers and migrants who cross a national border need to have the correct legal documents, such as passports, visas and permits.

## Refugee or asylum seeker?

According to the United Nations, a refugee is someone who has had to leave their country because of war, violence or persecution. Sometimes people are forced to flee from one part of their home country to another. As they do not cross a national border, they are known as internally displaced persons (IDPs) rather than refugees, although they may face many of the same hardships.

When a refugee reaches a country where they hope to gain safety, they may ask for 'asylum' (protection), or the right to remain in the new country. Once a refugee starts this legal process, they are called an 'asylum seeker'. If the government of the new country decides the person is genuinely a refugee, and that the country's immigration rules have been met, the refugee is given 'refugee status' and allowed to remain. If asylum is refused, the person may be deported (forced to leave the country) or they may become an undocumented immigrant (see page 5).

A mother and her son, refugees from the Syrian Civil War, wait at a camp for refugees in Greece in 2015.

## Citizen or stateless?

A citizen of a country is someone who is a legal member of that state. Citizens have the right to vote, work and claim healthcare. A person usually has citizenship of a country automatically, because they were born there. In many countries, it is possible to gain citizenship because a parent is a citizen, or by marrying a citizen. It is also sometimes possible to become a 'naturalised citizen' by living in the country for a certain number of years.

Some people hold citizenship of more than one country, while some are citizens of none. For example, 'stateless' people may be the children of refugees who have not been allowed citizenship of their new country.

## Why people emigrate

There are two sets of reasons why people emigrate: pull factors, which attract them to another country; and push factors, which drive them from their home country. Pull factors include the hope of more or better-paid jobs, or a better education. Other pull factors are emotional, such as joining family members or getting married. Some people emigrate looking for a better climate or a more relaxed lifestyle.

A major push factor is war. People may also emigrate because of persecution, when a particular group is treated badly. Sometimes, oppression may be widespread, as when a dictator limits the rights of all citizens. Other push factors are disasters, from earthquakes to famines, or a lack of natural resources, such as clean water.

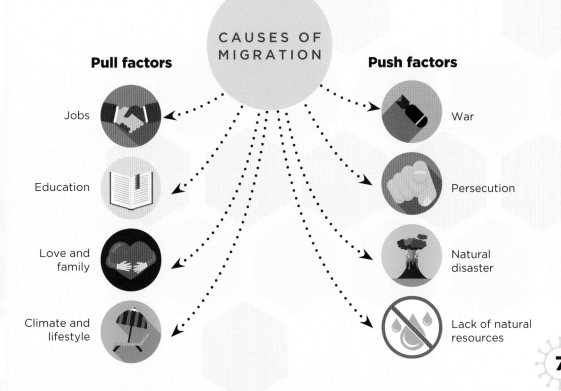

CAUSES OF MIGRATION

**Pull factors**

Jobs

Education

Love and family

Climate and lifestyle

**Push factors**

War

Persecution

Natural disaster

Lack of natural resources

## Barriers to migration

Alongside the factors that cause international migration are factors that prevent migration. A key barrier to migration is immigration laws, which may prevent a migrant from entering their desired new country. Some potential migrants may be discouraged by having to leave behind their family and community. Others may fear having to face prejudice or isolation in the new country.

Another barrier is the cost of the journey to the new country. In addition, for those who are forced to flee their country suddenly, or who leave home without the legal documents to enter their desired country, the journey may hold dangers if the need to travel immediately or secretly leads them to use unsafe or overcrowded transport. Other risks include physical barriers, such as seas, rivers and mountains, and the hazards of trying to avoid border guards.

## BARRIERS TO MIGRATION

Immigration laws

Cost of the journey

Dangers of the journey

Loss of family and community

Fear of prejudice

Fear of isolation

# CASE STUDY

## 'Coyote' people smugglers

People smugglers secretly transport undocumented migrants into another country, often putting the lives of migrants at risk. 'Coyotes' (named after the wolf-like animal of North and Central America) is the name for the people smugglers who work on the border of the United States and Mexico. In 2015, around 200,000 people successfully crossed from Mexico to the USA illegally, looking for a better or safer life. Many others were caught and turned back. In the same year, 240 migrants died crossing the border, from dehydration, heat stroke, drowning in rivers and canals, and car accidents. Coyotes take up to £3,000 from each migrant who is hoping to cross. People smugglers work all around the world, on any route where there are undocumented migrants. For example, an undocumented migrant hoping to travel from China to the UK or USA may pay people smugglers up to £38,000.

Coyotes transport undocumented Mexican migrants to a drop-off point, from where they must hike across the desert to the border with the USA.

## What can you do?

Try reading books and news articles aimed at young people about immigration and refugees to learn more about the issue. Take note of how people use terms like 'immigrant', 'asylum seeker' and 'refugee' and whether they use them correctly.

Modern humans evolved in Africa then migrated across the world. Before the development of countries, each with their own government and borders drawn on maps, immigration would not have been discussed in the same terms as today. However, the story of humankind has always been one of migrations.

### Early migrations

From the earliest days, human tribes have controlled territories. Conflict with other tribes, or the desire for more land and resources, has often led one group of people to press into the territory of another. For example, from the eighth century, desire for land led the Vikings, who were from Denmark, Norway and Sweden, to set up colonies in the British Isles, France, Iceland, Greenland, Russia and, briefly, North America. When these regions were already inhabited, there was intense conflict with the native population. In England, that conflict continued until the eleventh century.

In the thirteenth century, the migration of the Mongol tribes from their homeland in Central Asia created a vast empire that stretched from China in the east to Poland in the west.

This painting shows Mongol horsemen battling the Oghuz Turks for control of their territory.

## The 'New World'

By the fifteenth century, European nations had developed streamlined ships and good enough navigation to sail across the world. The Spanish, Portuguese, English, French and Dutch set up colonies in the Americas, which they called the 'New World', although it was already home to perhaps 50 million people. The settlers had a range of aims, from gaining freedom from religious persecution, to farming the vast areas of land and controlling local natural resources, including silver and gold.

## NATIVE POPULATION OF THE AMERICAS AFTER THE ARRIVAL OF EUROPEANS

As the European population of the Americas grew, the native population shrank: it is estimated that more than 80 per cent were killed by European diseases such as smallpox, as well as by conflict.

This memorial to the victims of the Irish Famine stands on the docks in Dublin, Ireland.

## CASE STUDY

### The Irish Famine

Between 1845 and 1852, the Irish Famine led to the emigration of around 20 per cent of the Irish population. The famine was largely due to the loss of the Irish potato crop, wiped out by a disease called blight. The disaster resulted in the deaths of around one million people. Another two million emigrated from Ireland. Most emigrants travelled to the United States and Canada. Tens of thousands died from disease in overcrowded ships on the Atlantic Ocean. Today, one in ten Americans, around 33 million people, say their ancestors came from Ireland.

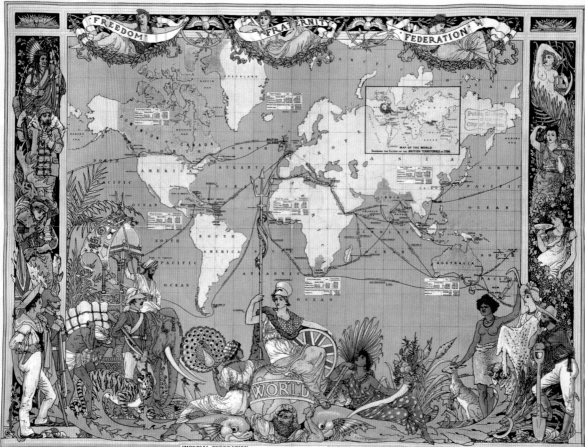

IMPERIAL FEDERATION. MAP OF THE WORLD SHOWING THE EXTENT OF THE BRITISH EMPIRE IN 1886.
STATISTICAL INFORMATION FURNISHED BY CAPTAIN J.C.R.COLOMB, R.P.FORMERLY R.M.A. ——— BRITISH TERRITORIES COLOURED RED

## Empire builders

Another great wave of migration took place in the late nineteenth century, when European nations competed with each other to colonise Africa. By 1914, the Belgians, British, French, Germans, Italians, Portuguese and Spanish had divided 90 per cent of African land between them. In some areas, large numbers of Europeans settled, changing African systems of government and ways of life for ever.

The British were in the process of building the largest empire since the Mongol Empire. By 1922, they ruled, and had settled in, almost a quarter of the Earth's land area, including Australia, Canada, India and South Africa.

This map, drawn in 1886, celebrated the British Empire, shown in pink. The small inset map shows the empire a century earlier. In 1886, the empire was still growing, with places such as Egypt, Kenya and Afghanistan yet to be addded.

## Protecting refugees

The Second World War (1939–1945) created the largest refugee crisis the world had seen: 60 million Europeans were refugees at some point. By 1951, one million of them had not found a place to settle. That year, the United Nations set up the Refugee Convention. This agreement laid down each country's obligation to take in refugees or send them to another country that had signed the agreement. Since then, 145 countries, out of the world's 195, have signed. The obligations were put to the test during further wars in the twentieth century. For example, the Vietnam War (1955–1975) led to around two million Vietnamese refugees seeking safety in the USA, France and elsewhere.

A Kindertransport child says goodbye to his mother.

# CASE STUDY

## The Kindertransport

Between 1938 and 1940, the UK took in around 10,000 Jewish children in a rescue known as the Kindertransport (German for 'children's transport'). The children were from Germany, as well as Austria, Czechoslovakia and Poland, which had been invaded by Nazi Germany under the leadership of Adolf Hitler.

In these countries, Jewish families were being sent to concentration camps. The UK government agreed that the children could come to live in UK homes, schools and foster homes, although their parents had to remain behind. Desperate to get their children to safety, parents put babies, toddlers and teenagers onto special trains. In most cases, these children were the only members of their family to survive the Holocaust, in which six million Jews were murdered.

## Palestinian refugees

One of the longest refugee crises is that of the Palestinians who became homeless after the 1948 Palestine War between the Jewish and Arab communities of Palestine. During the conflict, around 711,000 Arab refugees moved from the new state of Israel to the territories of the West Bank and Gaza Strip, and countries such as Lebanon, Syria and Jordan. Those refugees, their children and grandchildren were never to return home.

Today, more than half the population of the city of Ramallah, in the West Bank, are Palestinian refugees.

### Workers needed

In the years after the Second World War, some wealthy countries did not have enough workers to fill all their jobs in factories, construction and farming. They invited temporary migrant workers or permanent immigrants to fill the gaps. People from poorer countries saw an opportunity for a better life, or an escape from war at home.

The USA welcomed farm workers from neighbouring Mexico. France received many immigrants from its former colonies of Vietnam, in Southeast Asia, and Algeria and Morocco, in North Africa.

In 1948, the British government passed a law giving the right to live and work in Britain to all citizens of former British colonies. Tens of thousands of people arrived in Britain from countries such as Jamaica in the Caribbean, India and Pakistan in Asia, and Kenya and Somalia in Africa. Many of those people filled jobs in public services, such as transport and hospitals.

From the 1960s, many of these wealthy countries found they had fewer job vacancies to fill, so they made stricter laws about who could settle.

14

## Close neighbours

In 1993, 12 European countries formed the European Union, giving European citizenship to all citizens of member countries. Within the borders of the Union, citizens could settle and work where they wanted. As more European countries joined the Union, some countries had higher immigration from countries in the group where there were fewer opportunities for well-paid work. For example, after Poland joined the Union in 2004, there was higher emigration from Poland to the UK, Germany, France and Ireland. Today, Polish is the UK's fourth most spoken language, after English, Scots and Welsh.

West Germany, desperate to rebuild after the Second World War, invited thousands of temporary workers in the Gastarbeiter ('guest worker') program. These Gastarbeiter, from Turkey, Greece and Spain, are in a metal-processing factory.

### What can you do?

Research the history of your area to find out how immigration has shaped it. You could research place names, local businesses or the languages spoken.

When considering immigration, it is useful to know the facts about where migrants come from, where they are going and how immigration laws affect these movements. It is also helpful to question whether there is more immigration today than in the past.

### Highest immigration

Countries that have plenty of well-paid jobs and welcoming immigration laws usually have high immigration. The countries in this group may change over time. In addition, a country that neighbours, or is 'friendly' with, a war-torn country is likely to have high immigration for a period. Today, the countries with the highest number of immigrants per year are: the United States, Germany, Russia, Saudi Arabia, the United Kingdom, the United Arab Emirates, Canada, France, Australia and Spain.

### Highest emigration

Countries have high emigration for a range of reasons, including war or a lack of well-paid jobs. However, the countries with high emigration are not always the poorest or most unsafe. They may be countries where it is common to 'better yourself' by going abroad for work or study. For example, there are currently 4.7 million UK emigrants abroad. Today, the countries with the highest emigration per year are: Syria, India, Bangladesh, China, Pakistan, Sudan, the Philippines, Indonesia, Spain and Mexico.

### Net migration

Net migration is the difference between the number of immigrants entering a country and the number of emigrants leaving. Countries that have higher immigration than emigration have positive migration. These countries are usually wealthier and peaceful. Countries that have higher emigration than immigration have negative migration rates. These countries are often poorer or at war. Countries where immigration and emigration are equal have 'balanced' migration.

# NET MIGRATION

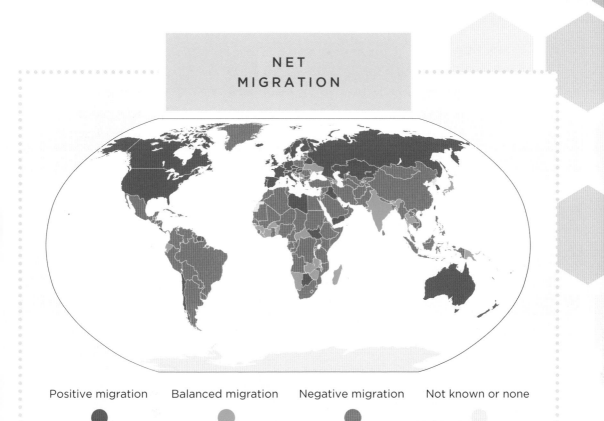

Positive migration ●    Balanced migration ●    Negative migration ●    Not known or none ○

## CASE STUDY

### Lithuania

Lithuania, in northeast Europe, is a country with high emigration and almost no immigration. While some countries worry about immigration, Lithuania is worried about emigration. Since 2004, when Lithuania joined the European Union (see page 15), around 370,000 Lithuanians have left, usually for other European countries. This has shrunk the population to 2.6 million. The reasons for emigration are low wages and struggling industries. Most of the emigrants are young and well qualified. This movement is often called a 'brain drain'.

## How many migrants?

According to the United Nations, in 2015, the number of international migrants (people living in a country other than the one where they were born) was 244 million. Just over three out of every 100 people was a migrant. Back in 2000, there were 173 million migrants. These figures show us that there is a growing number of migrants in the world because migration continues year after year. There is a movement of people going home, but it is a much slower trickle.

## Is global migration increasing?

Around the world, is the number of people who emigrate each year going up? Between 1990 and 2000, around two million people emigrated each year. Between 2000 and 2010, that number went up to 4.6 million every year. There are many possible reasons for this increase. For example, wars in Iraq and Afghanistan created millions of refugees. The world was becoming more globalised. 'Globalisation' is the process of the world becoming more interconnected as we trade and travel. However, in 2008, there was a worldwide financial crash, causing banks to collapse and many jobs to be lost in the world's wealthier countries. The result was a slowdown in migration, but the numbers increased again as economies recovered.

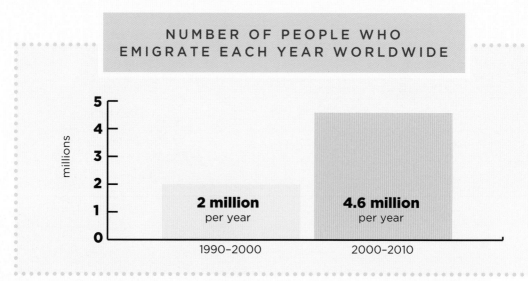

**NUMBER OF PEOPLE WHO EMIGRATE EACH YEAR WORLDWIDE**

millions

5
4
3
2
1
0

**2 million** per year — 1990–2000

**4.6 million** per year — 2000–2010

## Laws about immigration

Laws about immigration vary from country to country, and change as opinions on immigration change. Most migrants cannot stay in a new country without a work permit or visa, which allows them to get a job. Most countries, including the UK, give work visas to those who already have a job offer from an employer. The UK, USA and many other countries also give work visas to people who are 'highly skilled' (with good qualifications or training) or who work in professions, such as healthcare, where workers are needed. While a member of the European Union, the UK automatically gave EU citizens the right to work. Most countries offer student visas to people who have a place at a university or college. Many countries, including the UK, allow an immigrant to apply for citizenship after living there for five years. Most countries allow refugees to seek asylum.

The city of Sydney has long been one of the main points of arrival for immigrants to Australia.

## What can you do?

Find out more about a country with high emigration. Consider how life in that country differs from life in your country.

Fleeing from war, hunger or persecution, refugees have to leave their home country. Some seek safety in neighbouring countries, while others make dangerous journeys across land and sea.

## How many refugees?

In 2016, the United Nations said that the number of refugees in the world had reached its highest level ever, with a greater number of displaced people even than during the Second World War. 'Displaced' people are unable to return home. In 2016, 65.3 million people were refugees, asylum seekers or internally displaced (for definitions of these terms, see page 6).

### DISPLACED PEOPLE IN 2016

In 2016, one out of every 113 people was a refugee, asylum seeker or internally displaced.

## Where do refugees come from?

In 2017, the countries from which the highest number of refugees fled were: Syria and Afghanistan in Asia, and Somalia, South Sudan and the Lake Chad Basin countries of Cameroon, Chad, Niger and Nigeria in Africa. Over years and decades, the regions with the highest number of refugees will change, as wars begin and natural disasters hit. Wars were the main cause of the refugee crises in Syria, Afghanistan and South Sudan. Drought and conflict led to the refugee crises in Somalia and the Lake Chad Basin.

## War

The greatest causes of refugee crises are wars, including civil wars, when citizens of the same country fight each other. For example, in 2001 the USA, UK and allies invaded Afghanistan to topple the country's rulers, the Taliban. The Taliban had links with Al-Qaeda, the terrorists that carried out the 11 September 2001 attacks on the USA. Although the USA and allies had removed most of their soldiers by 2014, a civil war between the new Afghan government and the Taliban continued. At least 31,000 Afghan civilians (people who are not fighting) died in the conflict between 2001 and 2016. By the end of 2015, there were 2.7 million Afghan refugees, most of them in neighbouring Iran and Pakistan, with others in countries such as Germany, the UK and the USA.

Syrian refugees reach the Greek island of Lesbos in a dinghy.

# CASE STUDY

### Escaping Syria

The Syrian Civil War began in 2011, when the army of Syria's president, Bashar al-Assad, shot people protesting against his rule. Up to 1,000 different groups of Syrian rebels, including the terrorist group ISIS (Islamic State of Iraq and Syria), started to fight against the army and each other. By 2016, the war had killed up to 400,000 people, while around six million had fled the country. Many journeyed to neighbouring Turkey, while others boarded overcrowded boats to cross the Mediterranean Sea. This sea journey is among the world's most dangerous: in 2016 alone, more than 5,000 migrants drowned in the Mediterranean. Syrians were not the only victims: others came from Afghanistan, Iraq, Nigeria and Eritrea.

## Persecution

Persecution of particular groups of people by the wider population, or by governments, has been one of the greatest causes of emigration. Persecution may cause a diaspora, when a group of people move beyond their homeland in large numbers. This was the case in 2016–2017 when tens of thousands of Rohingya people fled Myanmar. At its most terrifying, persecution takes the form of genocide, which is the killing of a large number of people of one religion or ethnic group. Another form of persecution is marginalisation, when a group is excluded and given fewer rights. In India, a marginalised group is the Dalits, who according to traditional beliefs about 'caste', or class, are treated by some as 'untouchable'. Hundreds of thousands of Dalits have emigrated to the UK, USA and elsewhere.

In Turkey, a Kurdish girl joins in celebrations for the Kurdish New Year festival, called Newroz.

## CASE STUDY

### Persecution of the Kurds

The homeland of the Kurdish people spreads across the borders of Iraq, Turkey, Iran and Syria. Kurds speak their own languages and follow their own traditions. Kurds have often come into conflict with, and met with persecution from, the governments of the countries in which they live. Between 1986 and 1989, the Iraqi government carried out genocide, killing 182,000 Kurdish civilians. Today, out of 30 million Kurds, two million live abroad, with 800,000 of them in Germany.

# CASE STUDY

## Drought in Somalia

In 2017, Somalia, in East Africa, had not seen rain since 2015. Without water, crops had withered and animals died. People were hungry, leaving them weak and at great risk of disease. They were drinking from any water source they could find, causing outbreaks of diseases carried in dirty water, such as cholera. This drought followed a famine in 2010–2012, which killed 260,000 people, and a civil war that has lasted since the 1980s. In 2017, there were at least 880,000 Somali refugees.

Around 245,000 Somali refugees lived in camps at Dadaab in neighbouring Kenya.

## Drought

Droughts are a key cause of emigration from the world's warmer regions. Direct results of drought are hunger and disease. In addition, regions that are frequently hit by drought, such as central Africa, are usually poorer, as lack of water and food prevents development. Conflict is more likely to erupt over access to food and water, and any other natural resources, such as diamonds and other minerals. Such conflicts can prevent help reaching those in need, resulting in lengthy refugee crises.

## Disaster

Disasters can be natural, such as earthquakes, volcanic eruptions and hurricanes. Others are manmade, such as a chemical spill that does long-term damage to a region. Sometimes emigrants choose to return when the area becomes safe again. For example, in 1995, the Soufrière Hills volcano on the small Caribbean island of Montserrat erupted. Two-thirds of the island's population was forced to emigrate, mostly to the UK. Only 1,200 people remained. By 2016, the population had gone back up to 5,000.

## Life in refugee camps

Refugee camps may grow up as refugees make shelters for themselves out of the materials they find. Some camps are set up by governments or charities. An immediate issue in a refugee camp is disease, which may spread quickly in cramped conditions and particularly if there is a lack of proper toilets and drinking water. If the crisis continues for a long time, as in the case of the Afghan and Somali refugee crises, those living in a camp may face being stateless (see page 7) and jobless for many years. According to the United Nations, half of refugees are children aged under 18. In a camp, children may not be able to go to school or plan for their future.

## CASE STUDY

### Calais 'Jungle'

From 1999, a camp of refugees and other migrants grew up near Calais, France, reaching a peak of 8,000 people. It came to be known as the 'Jungle'. The migrants were hoping to cross the nearby English Channel to the UK. Some attempted to cross without the necessary documents by stowing away on ferries or on trains through the Channel Tunnel. The French and UK governments made attempts to 'process' the migrants to allow refugees and children the chance to claim asylum. The migrants' situation was not helped by disagreement between the French and UK governments over who should take responsibility.

In 2016, the French government cleared the Calais 'Jungle', moving some people to other camps or refugee centres.

## Life abroad

For refugees who seek asylum abroad, there are many problems to overcome. While seeking asylum, a refugee often has limited rights to healthcare and may not be allowed to work. If their claim for asylum is rejected but they are unable to return home, they can find themselves relying on charity or working illegally. Once a refugee has been given refugee status, they need to find work. Refugees can find their qualifications are not recognised, leading some doctors and teachers to take work as cleaners or shelf stackers. As they look for a permanent home, children may be moved from school to school, repeatedly facing the difficulties of making new friends. All these problems are worsened if refugees face hostility from people in the new country.

A police officer takes care of a young Syrian refugee while her family try to claim asylum at the German border.

### What can you do?

Find out more about the work of charities that help refugees, such as the Red Cross and Red Crescent. If you would like to help, try organising a school fund-raising activity.

**Some migrants go abroad in search of a better life. They may be economic migrants, who settle abroad for work or opportunities; or they may be social migrants, who move to be close to family or friends, or for a different lifestyle.**

### In search of work

Much economic migration is from poorer countries, where there are fewer well-paid jobs, to wealthier countries, where the pay is higher. However, this is by no means always the case. High-skilled migrants from wealthy countries may migrate for a better job. Every year, around a quarter of migrants are moving from one wealthy country to another. In addition, as many as four out of ten migrants move between neighbouring poorer countries to pursue work. In many countries, economic migrants play a large part in the economy. Saudi Arabia is very dependent on its foreign-born workers: 66 per cent of employees were born in a different country. In the UK, only 16 per cent were.

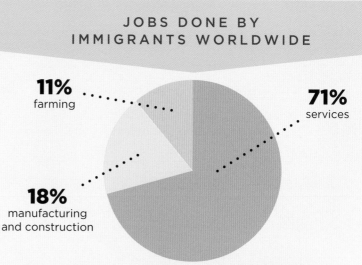

## JOBS DONE BY IMMIGRANTS WORLDWIDE

**11%**
farming

**71%**
services

**18%**
manufacturing and construction

Over 70 per cent of immigrant workers are employed in providing services, including domestic work, healthcare, banking and computing.

## Not staying for long

Not all economic migrants intend to stay in the new country for long. Short-term migrants range from highly paid businesspeople to low-paid fruit-pickers. For example, UK footballers such as Gareth Bale and Ashley Cole can be paid thousands of pounds a week to play for a club in Spain or the USA for a few seasons. Their situation is very different from that of migrants who are looking for low-skilled and low-paid jobs.

Low-paid jobs are often in farming, construction, factories or domestic work. Around 8.5 million female migrants find domestic work as nannies and housekeepers. While some of these migrant workers have short-term work visas, others are undocumented. As low-paid migrants have fewer legal rights than citizens, and even fewer if they are undocumented, they are at risk of being exploited or abused by employers.

## CASE STUDY

### Filipino migration

The Philippines is an island country in Southeast Asia. It has one of the world's highest rates of emigration, made up mostly of economic migrants. Around eight million Filipinos – nearly 10 per cent of the country's 85 million people – live abroad. The push factors are high unemployment and poor living standards. In the past, the Filipino government has encouraged emigration. Most Filipinos are short-term migrants, with many taking domestic work in countries such as Saudi Arabia and the United Arab Emirates.

These women were two of the sixty Filipino migrant workers living in this house in Qatar.

## Sending money home

A remittance is money sent home by an immigrant worker. Many immigrant workers make use of higher wages overseas to send money to their family at home to pay for food, education, healthcare and housing. In some countries, it is common for a mother or father to travel abroad alone to find work. Their remittance may be the family's only income. In 2015, US$582 billion was sent home.

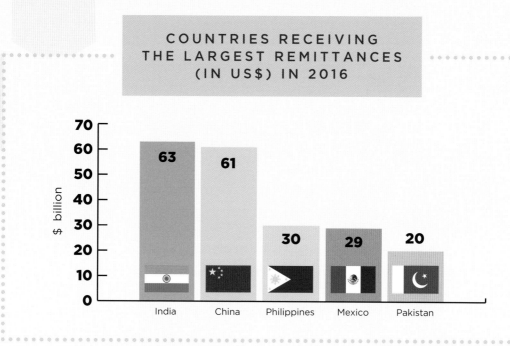

COUNTRIES RECEIVING THE LARGEST REMITTANCES (IN US$) IN 2016

## Searching for an education

Some families migrate in the hope of a better education for their children. This may be the case in countries where there are not enough schools or trained teachers, or where girls have fewer opportunities than boys. For example, around one in every three children in Afghanistan is not in school because there is no local school for them to go to. Most of these families cannot afford to emigrate, while for others the lack of education is added to the push factors (see page 7) that cause their migration.

# CASE STUDY
## Wild geese dads

Around 40,000 South Korean schoolchildren attend school abroad, usually in English-speaking countries such as the USA and UK. While mothers usually migrate with their children, the fathers remain in South Korea. South Korea is a wealthy country in Asia, home to brands such as Samsung and Hyundai. This growing band of fathers have become known as *kirogi appa*, or 'wild geese dads', due to the birds' long-distance migrations. While the families regret the separation, their aim is to make their children fluent in English and to give them the greatest possible opportunities.

The city of Seoul, South Korea, is home to many 'wild geese dads'.

## International students

About four million university or college students were born in a country other than the one where they study. Many international students are hoping to gain highly paid jobs when they return home, while some choose to stay in the host country. Many countries welcome international students, as their skills are likely to be a benefit in the long term.

### DESTINATIONS AND HOMELANDS OF INTERNATIONAL STUDENTS

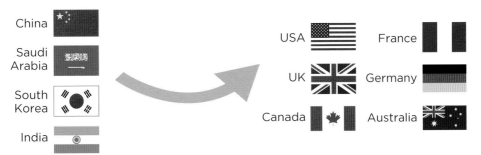

International students often head for English-speaking countries like the USA, UK, Canada and Australia.

## Retirement migration

Some people decide to emigrate when they retire. These people are social migrants. They may be attracted to another country by warmer weather, a relaxed lifestyle or a lower cost of living. If living costs, such as the prices of housing and food, are lower in the new country, then pensions and savings will stretch further. Some retired people may settle abroad to be closer to children and grandchildren who have already emigrated.

Most British retirees to Spain move to the coast, as well as warm islands such as Tenerife, Majorca and Menorca.

# CASE STUDY

## Retiring to Spain

Around 70,000 British retired people live in Spain, one of the most popular destinations for UK retirees. In contrast, in 2016 there were only 62 Spanish retirees living in the UK! Spain has a sunnier climate and lower house prices than the UK. Many retirees move to areas that are already popular with British people, such as the Costa del Sol ('Sunshine Coast'), where they will have English-speaking company. Local people sometimes complain that British retirees do not mix fully, or integrate, with the Spanish community. Another issue is that when an area has many elderly people, extra pressure is put on doctors and hospitals.

# FAMILY MIGRATION

Out of every 10 immigrants to the UK, 1 or 2 are joining family members.

## Moving for love

An international marriage is a marriage between two people from different countries. The couple may meet when one is holidaying, studying or working abroad. Sometimes, couples meet on the Internet. Citizens who were born abroad, or whose parents were, sometimes return to their homeland to find a wife or husband, or have a marriage arranged by family members, before bringing the new spouse back. In addition, families often migrate to join a family member, usually a father or mother, who has already found work and a home overseas. Immigration laws usually allow married couples and families to reunite, although the process of seeking citizenship may be difficult.

International marriages are a key cause of migration.

## What can you do?

Find out how you can support charities that help to provide education in the world's poorer regions. You could start by looking into the Malala Fund or Action Aid.

# IMMIGRATION

Some people worry that immigration is damaging, while others believe it is a benefit. Since immigration has always shaped our world, it is difficult to consider how life would be without it. However, it is possible to consider people's worries while weighing up the facts.

### Pressure on jobs?

In many countries, native workers worry that immigrant workers take jobs they could be doing. In some countries with high immigration, such as the UK, USA and Germany, around four or five people out of every 100 do not have a job. Is that because immigrants are taking jobs away from natives? Usually, that is not the case. Immigrants often fill gaps in the native workforce. Some take low-paid jobs in fields and factories that native workers do not apply for. Others take skilled jobs for which the country does not have enough trained workers. For example, more than a third of computer programmers in the USA's famous 'Silicon Valley' were born abroad.

However, low-skilled jobs (which need less training) may be more affected by immigration than high-skilled jobs. In some regions in a country, there are fewer jobs and most of them are low-skilled. If many low-skilled immigrants arrive, native workers may feel threatened, even if they are not directly losing their jobs.

Some immigrant workers do tiring and low-paid work.

## Pressure on pay?

Some people express concern that immigration lowers wages for everyone, because they think immigrants are willing to work for less money. For many high-skilled jobs, there is a set salary, so a doctor or designer born in Pakistan earns no less than a doctor or designer born in the UK. However, for low-paid jobs and work that is paid in cash, such as cleaning or gardening, there may be an effect on pay. Some recent immigrants may accept less money, because they are keen to find work at any cost. In the short term, this may push down wages for particular jobs.

However, many studies show that immigration boosts economies, which pushes up wages for everyone. Immigrants, in both low-skilled and high-skilled jobs, are often hungry for success. They tend to create jobs and wealth, as they are more likely than natives to start new businesses. In the UK, three times more immigrants than natives start their own businesses.

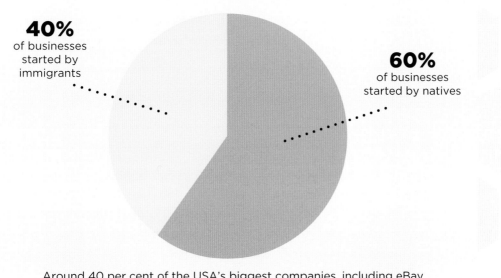

## FOUNDERS OF THE USA'S BIGGEST BUSINESSES

**40%**
of businesses started by immigrants

**60%**
of businesses started by natives

Around 40 per cent of the USA's biggest companies, including eBay and Google, were started by immigrants or their children.

## Pressure on services?

Some people worry that immigration puts pressure on public services, such as schools, hospitals and transport. In a country with a positive migration rate (see page 16), if a growing number of people need to use public services, there could be a shortage of school places or longer to wait for operations. However, since most adult immigrants pay taxes, which pay for public services, an answer is for governments to put more money into services so they can expand to fit the growing population.

In fact, many immigrants work in public services. In the UK, for example, more than a quarter of doctors were born abroad. Undocumented migrants cannot use public services or claim government money, called 'welfare' or 'benefits', as that would draw attention to their existence.

Some people fear that high immigration could lead to longer waits to see doctors.

## Assimilation?

Assimilation is when an immigrant or a group of immigrants adopts the language, dress and culture of their new country. In other words, the immigrant starts to 'fit in'. People may assimilate quickly if they come from a country with a similar culture. Sometimes an immigrant never fully assimilates, but their children do. Some people think that complete assimilation is a good thing. Others do not think someone should have to give up their own culture or dress. For example,

British people who retire to Spain (see page 30) often do not assimilate fully.

How quickly a person or group assimilates can affect how well they are tolerated by the country's natives. However, in countries that do not have a welcoming attitude towards immigrants, an immigrant may find it hard to assimilate. They will not be able to make the friendships that would allow them to learn new customs.

## Multiculturalism?

Multiculturalism is the idea that different cultures should live side by side in a country, with everyone treated equally and yet celebrating their differences. To encourage multiculturalism, governments in countries such as Britain and Sweden have often passed laws to try to make sure everyone is treated equally. In schools, children are encouraged to celebrate the festivals of different immigrant communities. However, some people argue that assimilation rather than multiculturalism should be encouraged. They think children should be taught more about the shared values of the country in which they live: the things that make 'Britishness' or 'Swedishness'.

In a multicultural society, everyone enjoys celebrating the festivals of other communities. Here, Chinese New Year is being celebrated in London.

## Isolation?

Sometimes a community of immigrants can be isolated, or cut off. In a new country, immigrants may feel happier if they live close to others who speak the same language. For this reason, some parts of a town or city may become popular with a particular community. Immigrants living there may even work in businesses run by friends and have little contact with the wider world. When a community is very isolated, the area is sometimes called a 'ghetto'. A problem with a ghetto is that it may limit the opportunities of people who live there. In addition, natives of a country may feel isolated if their local area has a large number of immigrants.

Brick Lane's many popular restaurants are run by London's Bangladeshi community.

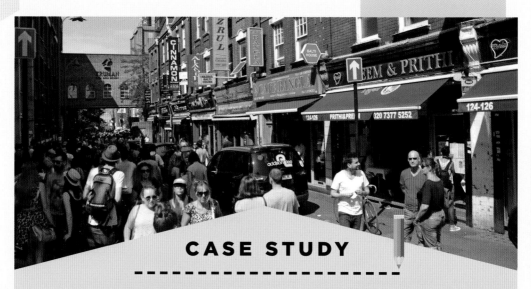

## CASE STUDY

### Brick Lane

Today, Brick Lane in London's East End is the centre of the UK's Bangladeshi community. The street is famous for its curry restaurants. One out of every three people living in the street and surrounding areas is Bangladeshi. Brick Lane has a history of being somewhere for new immigrants to settle, often in isolated communities. In the past, Brick Lane was close to London's docks and to many industries where immigrants could work, usually in low-paid jobs. In the seventeenth century, French Huguenots settled in Brick Lane, fleeing from religious persecution at home. In the nineteenth century, Irish and Jewish immigrants arrived. Today those communities have spread across the UK and play a role in every part of British society.

## Changing identities?

A person's identity, or their sense of who they are, may be linked to their nationality and their country's traditions. When an immigrant settles in a new country, they may be happy to take on new traditions and become 'British' or 'American' or 'Australian'. Some immigrants stick to their old identity, always feeling they are American, for example, even though they have lived in Japan for decades. The children of immigrants may also feel unsure about their identity. For example, their parents may encourage the stricter behaviour of their homeland, while their schoolfriends encourage them to break those rules. A child can wonder whether they are Pakistani or British, Korean or Australian.

At the same time, the character of the host country can begin to change as new languages are heard, new places of worship are built and new restaurants and shops open. While many natives welcome the opportunity to try new foods and make new friends, others worry about their own identity and try to preserve their own native traditions.

These New Yorkers are keeping alive Indian traditions by performing a Bhangra dance.

## Terrorism?

When people worry about a link between immigration and terrorism, they are usually thinking about militant Islamist terrorism against people in the USA and Europe, although there are many other forms of terrorism. Militant Islamists are people who use violence to pursue their extreme interpretation of Islam, an interpretation that is condemned by most Muslims. One large militant Islamist group is ISIS.

Some of the terrorists who have carried out attacks in Europe and the USA were immigrants, while others were born in the country they attacked. Would preventing immigration stop further attacks? Some say that such a harsh move would only fuel the anger that leads some people to be drawn to militant Islamism. Instead, some people argue, we should show more tolerance towards each other, both at home and abroad, making sure that everyone has equal opportunities. At the same time, many people think it is essential to end conflicts such as the Syrian Civil War, which has led to lawless regions where groups such as ISIS can grow (see page 21). This is not to say that excuses can ever be made for those who decide to kill innocent men, women and children.

Young British Muslims protest against terrorism after an attack in London in March 2017.

### Hate crime

A hate crime is a crime carried out against someone because of prejudice, perhaps because they have a different religion, were born in a different country or they are disabled. Hate crimes can be violent attacks or they can take the form of graffiti or bullying. Every year in the UK, several thousand hate crimes are directed against immigrant communities. One example of a hate crime took place in Croydon, London, in 2017 when a group seriously injured a Kurdish teenager (see page 22) after he said he was seeking asylum.

## The impact of immigration

### Tolerance?

Another impact of immigration may be tolerance, which is when people accept other's differences. Large cities that are used to high levels of immigration are often very tolerant places, particularly if different communities in the city mix with each other rather than living in separate areas. Although some people in Europe and the USA say they would like to see a drop in immigration, their behaviour towards immigrants they meet is usually respectful and supportive – it is racism that is usually not tolerated.

People take part in an anti-racism march.

### What can you do?

Research the festivals, food, religion and culture of a different local community. Ask a friend if you can join in with a family festival or visit their place of worship.

# Arguing about

## IMMIGRATION

**In recent years, immigration has become a bigger cause of argument in the USA and countries in Europe that have high immigration. Some people are worried by immigration, while others worry that not enough is done to help refugees from conflicts in Syria and Afghanistan.**

### Arguing against immigration

By the start of the twenty-first century, some political parties, such as the UK's British National Party (BNP), had been arguing against immigration for decades. These parties are what is called 'far right', or sometimes 'extremist'. Many people called them 'racist'. They did not usually get enough votes to play a role in government. However, things started to change in the twenty-first century as people who did not consider themselves 'far right' or 'racist' worried about the possible impacts of high immigration (see pages 32 to 39). This led to the growth of new parties that focused on tightening immigration laws, such as Alternative for Germany, and the rise of older anti-immigration parties, including the UK Independence Party (UKIP) and Freedom Party of Austria.

## EFFECTS OF WORRIES ABOUT IMMIGRATION

Worry about increase in immigration

**+**

Worry about decrease in jobs

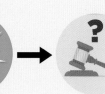
Rise in anti-immigration politics

Changing immigration laws?

## France's Front National

In 1972, Jean-Marie Le Pen founded the Front National political party in France. It was a 'nationalist' party, which meant it wanted to put the needs of native people first, and it was strongly opposed to immigration. Le Pen was found guilty in court of making racist statements. When Le Pen's daughter, Marine, took over the party leadership in 2011, she softened the party's image by voicing respect for immigrant communities while campaigning to control immigration. In the 2017 French presidential elections, Marine Le Pen came second, winning 34 per cent of the vote.

## Building walls

Noticing that anti-immigration ideas were growing popular, some politicians from 'mainstream' parties started to talk about tightening immigration laws. Some governments started to do it. In 2016, Donald Trump of the Republican Party, one of the USA's two main parties, was voted president. He promised to build a wall on the border with Mexico to prevent undocumented immigrants entering the USA.

Marine Le Pen opposes immigration. 'Au nom du peuple' means 'In the name of the people'.

When campaigning to become president, Donald Trump promised to reduce immigration to the USA.

## Brexit

In 2016, the UK government asked people to vote on whether they wanted to remain in the European Union. The country voted to leave by 52 to 48 per cent. This came to be known as Brexit (for 'Britain's exit'). The vote was widely seen as having a lot to do with fears about immigration: some people hoped that by leaving the EU, the UK would prevent citizens of other European countries from settling in the UK without a visa.

Hope Not Hate encourages neighbours to come together.

## CASE STUDY

### Hope Not Hate

Hope Not Hate is a UK organisation that campaigns against groups that it believes encourage racism, such as the BNP. Hope Not Hate has also campaigned against more mainstream politicians when it believes they use hurtful language to talk about immigration. In summer 2017, the charity helped to organise street parties across the UK, called the Great Get Together, encouraging people to celebrate all the UK's communities.

## Arguing for immigration

While some voters and political parties are opposed to immigration, some voters, parties and movements are just as strongly in favour of it. In particular, after 2011 some groups campaigned to make sure that their country did its duty towards the millions of refugees from the Syrian Civil War who had no option but to live in camps across Europe and the Middle East.

Although under international law these refugees were safe from being forced to return to war-torn Syria, not enough countries were offering to give enough of the refugees a permanent home. Despite pressure from parts of their population to do the opposite, governments of countries such as Germany, led by Angela Merkel, offered to welcome many hundreds of thousands of Syrian refugees.

# CASE STUDY

## Refugees Welcome

Refugees Welcome is a campaigning group with branches in many countries, including the UK. Each country's group campaigns for its government to give asylum to more refugees. It may also campaign for local councils to offer housing to refugees. In addition, it organises local volunteers to help and advise refugees after they have arrived in the country, even inviting refugees to stay in their homes. Members of the group also like to work with schools, helping children to know how best to welcome child refugees.

Child refugees attend a welcome party in the Netherlands.

## What can you do?

Find out about the views on immigration of the political party represented by your local MP. If you disagree with that policy, write a letter to your MP politely explaining why. Ask a parent, carer or teacher to read your letter before you send it.

# THE FUTURE

What does the future hold for refugees and for economic and social migrants? Will some countries close their borders to immigration? Will immigration continue to rise? Could the world respond to the current challenge of immigration in other ways?

### An equal world?

In the first two decades of the twenty-first century, it seemed as if many countries were tightening their immigration laws, setting extra tests and barriers for economic and social immigrants. If this continues, it might calm the fears of those in wealthy countries who want to protect their jobs and services. However, it would also see many citizens of poorer countries facing extra hardships, and citizens of wealthier countries having fewer opportunities if they are unable to work, study or retire abroad.

A great deal of economic migration is caused by inequalities, leading people to migrate from poorer countries to wealthier ones. If wealthy countries want to reduce immigration, then another option is to continue to work towards everyone having access to water, healthcare, schools and jobs in their homeland. Accomplishing this is probably the biggest challenge the world faces.

This tap in Mali, Africa, was provided by a charity. Worldwide, 884 million people do not have access to clean water.

## A safe world?

Since 1951, 145 of the world's countries have recognised their duty to give a safe place to refugees (see page 13). Today, under pressure from the many millions of refugees from wars in the Middle East and Africa, some countries are failing to face up to their duty as well as others, leaving many refugees to be passed from country to country or to remain stateless and homeless. In the long term, perhaps the only answer is for the world to work together to prevent wars, persecution and genocide before millions become refugees.

(see page 13)

## CASE STUDY

### The United Nations

The United Nations organisation was founded in 1945, immediately after the Second World War, to help countries to work together and to prevent conflicts. Today, 193 countries are members. The organisation frequently sends out soldiers to keep the peace, including in Syria and South Sudan, and distributes food and medicine after disasters. It puts pressure on countries that are oppressing their civilians. However, the UN is often held back from action by disagreements among its members, and concerns about how best to intervene in civil wars. Many people think the UN has a key part to play in the future of immigration. Could the UN do more to stop the push factors that make people emigrate, and put more resources into evening out global inequalities?

United Nations peacekeepers patrol Chad, in Africa, during violence between rebel groups in 2009.

### ?. What can you do?

Carry out a poll among family and friends to find out their views on immigration. Use the information you have learned in this book to start discussions, while being respectful of others' opinions and worries.

# GLOSSARY

**assimilation** – adapting to the way of life in a new country

**asylum seeker** – a refugee who has started the legal process of asking for protection in a new country

**citizen** – a legal member of a country, with full rights and responsibilities

**colonies** – territories settled and ruled by a foreign group

**concentration camps** – places where large numbers of people were imprisoned or put to death

**drought** – a long period without rain

**economic migrants** – people who settle in another country for work, higher pay or greater opportunities

**emigrant** – a person who leaves their country of birth, intending to settle abroad

**empire** – a number of countries ruled by one leader or country

**extremist** – a person who holds views that most people think are unacceptable

**European Union** – a group of European countries that share some decisions and work closely together

**famine** – an extreme shortage of food

**foreign worker** – a person who is invited to work abroad, usually in a skilled job

**Holocaust** – the murder of Jews and others by Nazi Germany during the Second World War

**illegal immigrant** – see undocumented immigrant

**immigrant** – a person who arrives in a new country, intending to settle there

**internally displaced person** – a person forced to flee from one part of their country to another, because of war or disaster

**low-skilled job** – a job that needs less training and is usually low paid

**migrant worker** – a person who moves to another country to look for work for a short period

**net migration** – the difference between the number of immigrants entering a country and the number of emigrants leaving it

**oppression** – cruel or unjust treatment by a government or ruler

**people smugglers** – people who illegally transport migrants from one country to another

**permit** – a document that officially allows a person to do something

**persecution** – cruel treatment, particularly because of a person's race or religion

**pull factors** – hopes and opportunities that draw people to another country

**push factors** – dangers and problems that cause people to leave their country

**refugee** – a person who has had to leave their country because of war, violence or persecution

**skilled job** – a job that needs a higher level of training or qualifications

**social migrants** – people who migrate for a better lifestyle or to be with family and friends

**stateless** – not a citizen of any country

**undocumented immigrant** – a person who has entered, or remains in, a country without legal permission

**United Nations** – international organisation that aims to create peace and co-operation

**visa** – a document or stamp in a passport that allows a person to enter, leave or remain in a particular country

# FURTHER INFORMATION

## Books

**Immigration (Ethical Debates)**
Cath Senker (Wayland, 2011)

**Kindertransport (Stories of World War II)**
AJ Stones (Wayland, 2015)

**Who Are Refugees and Migrants? What Makes People Leave Their Homes?
And Other Big Questions**
Michael Rosen and Annemarie Young (Wayland, 2016)

## Websites

Find out more about immigration and refugees on these websites:

http://www.iamsyria.org/
Information and teaching resources about refugees from the civil war in Syria

http://www.unhcr.org/uk/
Read about the work of the UN Refugee Agency and the current situation for refugees
around the world

https://www.refugeecouncil.org.uk/
Find out about the work of the UK's Refugee Council charity and how you can help

# INDEX

# OUR WORLD IN CRISIS

9781445163710   9781445163734   9781445163772   9781445163758   9781445163819   9781445163796

W
FRANKLIN WATTS
LONDON•SYDNEY